The oyster men

For generations, many old Cornish families have fished for oysters on the Carrick Roads and the surrounding rivers. Governed by laws that dictate to preserve the natural environment of the river beds, the last remaining oyster men still fish by long established methods, using sail power and hand pulled dredges. These waters form the last traditional oyster fishery in Europe – and the men and their sail boats pursuing this hard living are now but few.

As a photographer, I recognised the importance in documenting this declining Cornish industry before it is lost forever. The oyster season runs from 1st October to 31st March and, armed with an ageing Rolleicord camera, I set out on a quest to capture a photographic archive of the oyster dredging community of today.

My aim was to provide a valuable insight into an industry that is part of the rich tapestry of Cornish life. At the same time, these images aim to salute the last men working on the fishery in the 21st century, and to stand as a tribute to their forebears.

Mal Stone, Falmouth 2005.

Above: Frank Vinnicombe and 'Shadow'.

Ada

Colin Frost began fishing for oysters after leaving school. Colin's father, Ray was an oyster man before him. For generations the Frost family have worked out of Restronguet Creek, Ray owning 'Stella' and Colin aboard 'Katherina', which is now owned and worked by Jonathan Bailey. In later years Colin bought 'Ada', a pilot boat from Hayle. Originally built in Porthleven, she spent many of her 120 years as a pilchard driver in St. Ives.

It was a bright, brisk winter morning when I headed out to the fishery on a borrowed oyster punt. There were eight gaff rigged boats dredging off the north bank. In the distance I observed the reddish 'bark' sails of 'Ada' silhouetted against the sunlit January sky. Dashing across the Carrick Roads, I managed to get a few shots of Colin dredging before he sailed back for the next drift. In the breeze he was soon gone. The wind was freshening fast as the waves began to show their white tops. Timmy Vinnicombe suggested I head for the sanctuary of Falmouth Harbour because the wind was getting up. I trusted his expertise implicitly. That was the first and last I saw of Colin that season.

Boy Willie

These fishermen types are hardy souls, I decided. It was early morning on Mylor Harbour. I was cold and wet, with my back to the torrid rain as I tried to protect my camera, which was wrapped in a couple of polythene bags. Timmy smiled as we set out to sea. He seemed totally impervious to the weather. That's probably because Timmy Vinnicombe's family have been in the fishing industry for five generations and his boat has seen about 150 years of sterling service. The 'Boy Willie' was a lugger pilchard driver. Built in Porthleven, she was an old boat when Timmy's grandfather bought her in 1923. Timmy's father George also spent a life under her sails until, as a tired old lady, she was laid up in Mylor Creek. In 1988 Timmy decided to race her. Through years of constant hard work she had fallen into such a grim state of disrepair that the Vinnicombes had to wrap her hull in cellophane in order to tow her to the repair yard on the Fowey River. Here at Golant, she would be lovingly restored to become an oyster dredger.

Boy Willie

On board with us this wet and miserable morning was John
Blackford. He religiously pulls a third dredge on 'Boy Willie'
every Saturday. John recalled his first oystering experiences back
to the early 70s, when he and an associate, Stevie Richardson,
worked a haul-tow punt in Mylor Creek. John and Timmy became
firm friends in the mid 80s whilst racing together on 'Evelyn'.
When Tim took John to Golant to show him the working boat he
planned to race, John could scarcely believe his eyes: "You could
see the beach straight through her hull," remarked John.
Together they spent the next six months rebuilding her to
pristine condition, and by 1989 she was ready to sail. As 1995
came, Timmy decided to fish for oysters and she was put back to
work. John began oyster dredging with Tim in 2003. 'Boy Willie'
is now the only large working boat in the fleet which races through
the summer months and fishes for a living during the winter.

Dolly

Barry Prynn began oystering in 1972, having been out only twice
on Frank Cock's boat 'Morning Star'. He bought 'Dolly' from
Frank's son, John, having had no sailing experience whatsoever.
It was a rough, grey and very choppy day when I met Barry and
Toby, his three legged black dog. Within an hour of dredging
I began to feel unwell. Barry immediately noticed my enthusiasm
was somewhat dampened. Barry shouted, "You're not feeling good
are you? Don't worry, we all get seasick. I'm always sick first day
I go fishing. Just make sure you're away from the windward side
and you'll be alright!" As the day passed, the bowsprit stopped
dipping into the water and the boat became more stable.
I managed to eat a sandwich and felt much better. By three o'clock
the tide was at its lowest as we sailed back to Mylor Harbour. Barry
handed me the tiller while he tidied the dredges and packed the
day's catch. Totally inexperienced, I was petrified I'd ground the
boat – I could feel the keel catching the sea bed. We picked up
the mooring on the first attempt. I was very relieved!

Iris Elizabeth

It was midday when I finally got onto the water. I'd spent all morning sitting on the wall at Mylor with the boys. Listening to Marshall Vinnicombe's yarns, drinking stewed tea and eating squashed sandwiches, we awaited a mere breath of wind to blow the sails. There wasn't an ounce of it around. With dull grey skies and just three hours left of the oyster man's day, Alun and I left the mooring on 'Iris Elizabeth' as a minute ripple of air finally caressed the water.

Alun Davis' career in the oyster industry began on leaving school over 40 years ago. Colchester oysters were his first catch before moving on to Whitstable with the Seasalter and Ham Oyster Fishing Company. They supplied over 60% of the UK market, but a move within the company to management trainee found young Alun based in Cornwall, until Macfisheries took them over in the early 70s. Alun left the company and began dredging with Kenny Corke on 'Evelyn' until procuring his own boat 'Florence', which he both worked and raced. The old girl was sold to the St. Mawes Syndicate after purchasing 'Iris' in 1997 from Norman Bowers.

A passionate man within the Truro Oyster Fishery, Alun campaigns for a fair deal for the oyster men. Having survived the Bonamia virus which ravaged the fishery for a decade, the plight now lies with the threat of massive licence increases. A few hours with Alun not only gave me a trip aboard another interesting vessel but also a valuable insight into what a delicate balance it is to keep the fishery alive in the 21st century.

Mistress

One crisp March morning I was waiting outside the Pandora Inn. Eventually John Cock arrived and we headed along Restronguet Creek through the thick muggy fog. Leaving the mooring, the old oyster man's cottage where he'd been born looked down on us through the mist. It seemed strange that 70 years later, his boat was moored just a stone's throw away. His father, Frank Cock, had been an oyster man all his life and John worked with him aboard their family boat, 'Morning Star'. Built circa 1820 in Portloe, Frank had bought her in 1947 and she'd faithfully served before being cruelly run down on her moorings one night in 1981, never to sail again. A double blow came with the discovery of the Bonamia virus on the fishery, so John turned to his trade as a shipwright. On retirement he bought 'Mistress', a Heard-built Mevagissey Tosher, and resumed oyster fishing.

Out on the Carrick Roads the fog hung low all day long. We got the occasional glimpse of Barry Prynn, ghosting through the mist as he sailed 'Dolly' back to her next drift. We knew she was out there somewhere because we could hear Barry's dog Toby barking every time the dredge was thrown overboard!

Rhoda Mary

Oyster man Roy Collins has fished along Mylor Creek for over half a century. His brother Rex, joined him in 1969 and dredged whenever he wasn't sea fishing for mackerel. Roy worked on Frank Vinnicombe's boat 'Boy Phil' for many years. Against all odds, during the Bonamia virus, he and Frank still tried to salvage the fishery. As a 14-year-old, young Rex would turn the winding gear on George Vinnicombe's haul-tow punt 'The White'. He reminisced, "I loved October 1st. There would be at least 16 punts in Mylor Creek, all waiting to go. Bunny Bennetts used to start the season with a shot gun, taking his cue from the pips on the radio. I know he had a gun, but I don't believe he owned any ammunition. I think George Vinnicombe used to give him the cartridges. Those were the days – now there isn't a single oyster in the creek."

In 1977 the two brothers undertook to build a boat of their own. Based on the lines of Frank Vinnicombe's 'Shadow' they constructed 'Rhoda Mary', a faithful replica up in the woods at Mylor. The local council took a dim view of proceedings, evicting the brothers and their boat for not having planning permission. A charitable Terry Heard allowed them to conclude the work in the lane outside his yard. During the last season, brother Roy's involvement was curtailed due to ill health. Thirty years on, 'Rhoda Mary' still graces the Carrick Roads with her presence although Rex now works her alone.

Shadow

Grey, cold, wet and windy days: are these forever the working environment of an oyster man? Not only did they pull freezing cold iron dredges from high 'spring' tides but also endured the most gruelling of weathers, chilling their joints to the bone.

One fisherman who has frequently braved such elements these past 70 years is Frank Vinnicombe. Now aged 84 and recovering from a hip replacement operation, I caught up with him on such a typical day aboard his boat 'Shadow'. Frank's career began aged nine when he first fished for oysters. Apart from a break between the ages of 18 and 23 when he fought in the Second World War, he has spent his lifetime on the fishery. His grandfather owned the 'Shadow', built in 1864 by Hitchens of Point, which Frank purchased from him in 1946. Brother George would occasionally join Frank, oystering on her when the elements were too cruel and dangerous to fish in the deep seas around the Cornish coastline. After the war, he and George often dredged up old shells of a very different nature found in the Carrick Roads!

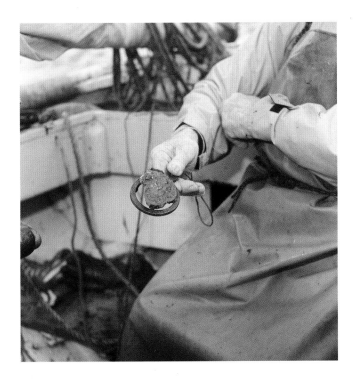

Shadow

Frank works the fishery each day accompanied by Tim Mayer, his apprentice of six years. Throughout our sail, Frank spoke of his life as an oyster man, amazing me with his knowledge of the fishery and the stories he could tell. Working his way across the bank, he would look towards Restronguet Point and shout, "We're going about." This was the signal to sail back for the next drift. Later he confided to me that when a certain tree eclipses Frank Cock's old house, he knows he's reached the end of the bank. The tides were high as the two men pulled dredge after dredge, brimming with oysters through the deep water.

Packing away the heavy dredging bars as we sailed back to the safety of Mylor Harbour, Tim reminded himself aloud to purchase some Paracetamol tablets. "Have you got a headache?" I asked. "No, just a broken collar bone," he replied. I'd never have guessed.

Six Brothers

Today was one of those damp days when the rain comes and goes every half an hour and you never get dry. As I sat on the gunnels of the 'Six Brothers', Marshall Vinnicombe pulled the heavy, cold dredges laden with oysters through fathoms of icy water while reflecting on his life and that of his seafaring family.

Their boat 'Six Brothers' was built at Feock by William Ferris in 1890. Previously owned by the six Lewarne brothers who lived on the Helford River, the boat was sold on the understanding that she would always be called 'The Six'. Marshall's father, George Vinnicombe, purchased the boat in 1953 and worked her as an oyster dredger. Sadly, during a storm in 1968 she broke her moorings at Mylor Harbour and smashed to pieces on Greatwood Quay, leaving only the transom and keel intact. George Vinnicombe was heartbroken. Through drawings produced by Percy Dalton, he had her rebuilt by Skettleberry's in Plymouth, and in 1969 she returned to Falmouth waters. During the mid 70s, Marshall and brother Timmy would race her during the summer months. Thirty years on, Marshall works her solely through the winter as an oyster dredger.

Swallow

Paul Ferris, the moorings officer at Truro Harbour Office kindly offered to assist this photographic project by forwarding my contact details to each oyster man who applied for an oyster dredging licence. One Saturday morning, a week prior to the start of the oyster season, I received a phone call from Kenny Corke. He was preparing his old gaff rigged cutter 'Swallow' in readiness for the gruelling winter ahead. She is an old girl now, showing all of her 114 faithful years as a working boat but still willing to pursue another five months hard labour.

Although I managed to speak with Kenny, I only saw him on the water while I was aboard 'Six Brothers'. Unfortunately, on days he was out, I wasn't, and vice versa. Kenny's father, George had been an oyster man, sailing on the 'Evelyn' – a boat which Kenny owned too, in later years. Eventually she was sold to the St. Mawes Syndicate after the Bonamia virus struck. Once the parasite had gone from the beds, the oyster fishing resumed and so did Kenny. He bought 'Carrie' – a Heard 23, before selling her to make way for 'Swallow' which he'd found on the upper reaches of the River Fal at Coombe Creek.

Due to retirement, this season would be Kenny's last, but the family tradition will prevail with son Rodney taking over to helm 'Swallow' in seasons ahead.

Three Sisters

Beside the harbour, the trees in Mylor Churchyard were whipping in the wind as Les Angell arrived in his old pick-up truck. Pulling on his wet weather gear I sensed another cold day ahead. As he hauled up the mainsail on 'Three Sisters', I leant against the side decks, still engulfed in yesterday's weed.

Leslie Angell was a mere neophyte aged 17 when he first began dredging for oysters. The old master, Frank Vinnicombe, his mentor, taking him aboard 'Shadow'. Working alongside Roy Collins on 'Boy Phil', another of Frank's boats, extended his experience further. He later moved on to work 'Helen Mary' with Ron 'Hammer' Laity, before buying 'Boy Phil' from Frank and going it alone. Finally, in a deal between himself and John Walls, 'Boy Phil' was succeeded by his current boat, 'Three Sisters'.

Heat burnt into my chest as I drank my flask of hot tomato soup. Les 'jibed' the boat with all his dredges out – a tactic he's perfected for catching any unsuspecting, passing scallops. The winter's bitter cold permeated my toes even though I sported three pairs of socks beneath my wellingtons. One o'clock arrived none too soon that Saturday.

Ghosts in the mist

Although I intended to cover every oyster man working the fishery over the season, I did not manage to capture them all. On days I was able to traverse the water, some oyster men weren't around. Unfortunately Bill Rogers and Jonathan Bailey escaped my prying lens: I could never catch Jonathan leaving Mylor Creek aboard 'Katherina', but hopefully I might make his acquaintance another season.

From the bottom of my heart, I can only but thank the oyster men I met on the fishery for their endearing hospitality. I was soon made welcome by everyone I met – they gave me a wonderful experience. Armed with my camera and a poly bag containing food plus my wet weather overalls, I'd sit on the bench overlooking Mylor Harbour. Some days would be frosty as the sunlight broke over Greatwood Quay. Other mornings it would be dark, dank and grey, barely making daylight. We'd stand waiting on windless mornings with nothing to drive the sails. John Blackford would feed sandwiches to the robins as the other boys discussed the quantity of yesterday's catch. My apologies to Marshall Vinnicombe for the lack of breeze on what must seem like every morning I appeared. Jokingly, he eventually started to ask me to ring if I was coming again so he could stay in bed: "I look out of my window, and if that tree at the bottom of my garden isn't quivering then it's not worth me coming out!" he'd say.

On days he wasn't there, Timmy Vinnicombe and the boys quipped of going and shaking his tree.

Without reservation I trusted Timmy's word. He always had everything summed up through his seasoned knowledge of the sea. "Wrap up all you can – you can always take stuff off. If you haven't got enough you'll always be cold." Simple yet sage advice. For the duration of this project, my life has revolved around whether it will rain, how many socks shall I wear and what sandwiches will I make to sustain me? What flavour of Campbell's soup shall I have today? And do I really want a hard-boiled egg in my pocket as I bounce atop the waves?

These were halcyon days when the winter sun shone bright, spilling long shadows from the mast onto the water as drab, buff, weathered sails took the wind, their sheets flapping as we'd 'go about'. Equally memorable was the smell of weed on the decks from clogged dredges; the rattle of the catch on cultch boards even as empty shells were returned to the deep. I now appreciate how infectious this way of life could become: I have come to understand these hardy men. In today's fragile environment, both natural and political, I pray for their continuing salvation.